BEGIN *Your* HEALING

Your Spiritual Healing Journal.
Your Letters to God.

E.J.H. MOFFETT

Begin your Healing by E.J.H. Moffett

ISBN 978-1-970072-71-6 (Paperback)
ISBN 978-1-970072-72-3 (Hardback)

This book is written to provide information and motivation to readers. Its purpose is not to render any type of psychological, legal, or professional advice of any kind. The content is the sole opinion and expression of the author, and not necessarily that of the publisher.

Scripture taken from the New King James Version®. Copyright © 1982 by Thomas Nelson, Inc. Used by permission. All rights reserved. Exceptions are noted as follows: English Standard Version (ESV), King James Version (KJV), and New International Version (NIV).

Copyright © 2019 by E.J.H. Moffett

All rights reserved. No part of this book may be reproduced, transmitted, or distributed in any form by any means, including, but not limited to, recording, photocopying, or taking screenshots of parts of the book, without prior written permission from the author or the publisher. Brief quotations for noncommercial purposes, such as book reviews, permitted by Fair Use of the U.S. Copyright Law, are allowed without written permissions, as long as such quotations do not cause damage to the book's commercial value. For permissions, write to the publisher, whose address is stated below.

Printed in the United States of America.

New Leaf Media, LLC
175 S. 3rd Street, Suite 200
Columbus, OH 43215
www.thenewleafmedia.com

Given with so much love

To _____

From _____

Written for my children, Eric, Harry II, and Leslie; for my grandchildren, Genesis, Zion, Trinity, Champion, Mike, Harrison and a grandchild due in 2020; because of my journey; and in loving and sacred memory of Big Harry.

> He hath hedged me in so that I cannot get out;
> He has made my chains heavy.
> Even when I cry and shout,
> He shuts out my prayer.
> He has blocked my ways with stone;
> He has made my paths crooked.
> *Meditate on Lamentations 3:7–9*

Are you surprised that these words appear in the Holy Bible? These verses come from the third chapter of Lamentations, the twenty-fifth of thirty-nine books in the Old Testament. In this passage, the prophet Jeremiah expressed the sorrow, grief, and helplessness he felt after God had chosen him to bring a message of "repentance from idolatry" to the Israelites. He felt hedged in and chained down. He felt unheard. He felt blocked by the very God who had called him for this work while he was still in his mother's womb.

Jeremiah wrote Lamentations in 586 BCE right after the fall of Jerusalem, the city where the life, death, and resurrection of Jesus Christ took place.

Jeremiah, one of four major prophets mentioned in the Holy Scriptures, will forever be known as the weeping prophet. He is called this because of his grief over the stubbornness of the people of Judah and because he saw the destruction that would befall Jerusalem, a profoundly important city even to this day. Jeremiah's emotions ran deep and caused his tears to flow often. He cared for his people and loved his country. He was a faithful servant. On Jerusalem's behalf, he asked, "Who can console you? Who can heal you?" He was troubled, and he would write to God.

> "How can I console you? To what shall I liken you, O daughter of Jerusalem?
> What shall I compare with you, that I may comfort you, O virgin daughter of Zion?
> For your ruin is spread wide as the sea; who can heal you?"
> *Meditate on Lamentations 2:13*

Why discuss Jeremiah's troubles in the first pages of this spiritual healing journal? Why focus on this one figure among all those written about in the Holy Scriptures? Jeremiah merits this attention because he was chosen by God and would obediently write to Him and ask for healing. He answered God's call during one of the darkest moments in Old Testament history. In the beginning, Jeremiah ran from his prophetic calling, but eventually he delivered God's message of judgment and destruction to the people. His message was so important that God commanded him to write it down. Jeremiah proclaimed all the words he received from God and had Baruch, the son of Neriah, write them on a scroll. The words God spoke to Jeremiah were written and still can be found in the scriptures.

> "Now it came to pass in the
> fourth year of Jehoiakim
> the son of Josiah,
> king of Judah,
> *that* this word came to
> Jeremiah from the Lord, saying:
> 'Take a scroll
> of a book and write on it
> all the words that I have
> spoken to you against Israel,
> against Judah,
> and against all the nations,
> from the day I spoke to you,
> from the days of Josiah
> even to this day.
> It may be that the house
> of Judah will hear
> all the adversities which I purpose
> to bring upon them,
> that everyone may turn
> from his evil way,
> that I may forgive their iniquity
> and their sin.'
> Then Jeremiah called Baruch
> the son of Neriah;
> and Baruch wrote on a
> scroll of a book,
> at the instruction of
> Jeremiah, all the words of the Lord
> which He had spoken to him.
> And Jeremiah commanded Baruch,
> saying, 'I *am* confined,
> I cannot go into the
> house of the Lord.
> You go, therefore,
> and read from the scroll
> which you have written
> at my instruction,
> the words of the Lord,
> in the hearing of the
> people in the Lord's house
> on the day of fasting.
> And you shall also
> read them in the hearing
> of all Judah who come
> from their cities.
> It may be that they
> will present their supplication
> before the Lord,
> and everyone will turn
> from his evil way.
> For great is the anger
> and the fury that the Lord
> has pronounced
> against this people.'
> And Baruch the son of
> Neriah did according
> to all that Jeremiah
> the prophet commanded him,

reading from the book the words of the LORD in the LORD's house.'"
Jeremiah 36:1-8

Jeremiah was called *to* speak *for* God. This spiritual healing journal will call you *to* speak *to* God so you can speak *for* God also. You are a part of that chosen generation written about in ***1 Peter 2:9***.

In ***Jeremiah 1:17***, God told Jeremiah to "gird up his own loins." Although He knew the answer, He was asking the prophet, What Hinders You. He was asking the prophet WHY. What keeps you from heeding My call to speak for Me? God again told Jeremiah that He had chosen him to speak to the Israelites about their wickedness, their idolatry, and their abandonment of Him. Eventually Jeremiah rose and spoke for God—just as you will.

You see, even in his youth, Jeremiah knew about the destruction of Jerusalem and the devastation that would come to his country, Judah. He hesitated and made excuses for **WHY** he could not heed God's call. One of his excuses was that he was only twenty years old and was simply too young.

Take a moment and think about your excuses. Which ones will you make? There should be no excuse for you not to heed the call to speak for God.

Jeremiah wrote to God just as you will write in your spiritual healing journal. He wrote about the destruction of Jerusalem. He cared about the people there and loved his nation. He was devoted to God. Please pay close attention to this fact: Jeremiah's troubles overwhelmed him when he chose **not** to speak for God.

> "For when I spoke,
> I cried out; I shouted,
> 'Violence and plunder!'
> Because the word of the Lord
> Was made to me a reproach
> and a derision daily."
> Then I said, "I will not make
> mention of Him, nor speak anymore
> in His name." But His word was in
> my heart like a burning fire
> shut up in my bones;
> I was weary of holding it back,
> and I could not".
> ***Meditate on Jeremiah 20:8–9***

What troubles you? Have you written to God about it? There is healing in writing. The men of God who wrote the Holy Scriptures wrote as God moved them. More than eighty scriptures include the words "it is written." The New Testament books from Romans to Jude are letters written to believers who were saluted with a holy kiss in the churches of Christ (***Romans 16:16***). These church members were simply called Christians (***Acts 11: 26***) and worshipped at one of the congregations (***Ephesians 1:22, 23***) of the only church (***Romans 12:5***) you can read about in the scriptures.

Some of the letters in the New Testament were written to a wider, more public group of church of Christ members. The book of Hebrews is formatted as a sermon but is really a letter written to restate and reinforce the superiority and importance of faith in God.

Some of the letters in the New Testament were more personally written, intimate messages. The book of Philemon was a personal letter written by the apostle Paul to his longtime friend Philemon. He wrote to ask him to forgive his runaway slave Onesimus, who was now a Christian and Philemon's brother in Christ. Writing is a powerful, far-reaching, personal, ever-lasting way to begin your healing.

Do you have an answer to your **WHY**? WRITE TO **GOD**. Discovering your **WHY** will bring with it agitation. Applying God's healing written words to your **WHY** will bring you to reconciliation. Just like Jeremiah, you will not be able to keep your words to yourself. They will be like a burning fire shut up in your bones (*Jeremiah 20:9*).

What troubles you? Are you experiencing a storm, or have you just emerged from one? Are you heading back into a storm? Stormy times will come.

Have you lost your job? Has the opportunity to work been taken from you?

Did a loved one die fifty-five days after a brain tumor was discovered, many cancers were found, and the physician called each of them aggressive?

Stormy times will continue to come. Do you have a child you love dearly that's addicted to opioids?

Are you overwhelmed by your debts and responsibilities?

Is someone you know gay, HIV positive, absent from the family, and causing your heart to break new everyday?

Are you lonely?

Are you uncertain?

Are you anxious?

Are you depressed?

Are you concerned about the troubles in your personal Jerusalem?

These hindrances are among the reasons passages like ***Lamentations 3:7–9*** are in the Holy Bible.

Just like Jeremiah, you should not ignore your **WHY**. Tell God. Tell Him when you can't tell anyone else. WRITE TO **GOD**. The things that break your heart break God's heart too. He already knows all about your heart breaks anyway.

Open your Bible. Go deep and wide inside its pages. Before writing to God, stay awhile in the Holy Scriptures. Really discover and mediate on the Word of God. You will find more answers than you could ever imagine. These answers will outnumber the questions you will ask because you will be in the presence of the God who is "able to do exceeding abundantly above all you ask or think, according to the power that works within you, to Him be glory in the church by Christ Jesus to all generations, forever and ever. Amen" (***Ephesians 3:20–21***).

Dear Heart,

The steadfast love of the Lord never ceases; His mercies never come to an end; they are new every morning; great is your faithfulness. "The Lord is my portion," says my soul, "therefore I will hope in Him." ***Apply Lamentations 3:22–23.***

Pray with me please. Help me to always talk to You through my prayers, my praise, and my letters to you God. Your grace and Your mercy will move each of us through our dark **WHY's**, through Your healing answers and into Your marvelous light. ***Study Psalm 139.***

BEGIN *your* **HEALING** ...
WRITE TO **GOD**.

Put your spiritual healing journal under your pillow.
When you cannot sleep,
Arise,
Write to God—
It's your soul He keeps.

a few fowers ™
30 September 2013
11:07 a.m.
The sky above my home at this moment in God's time.

You can ask God anything. He answers every prayer.

Today's **WHY**

_____   _____
   The Day   The Date

Dear God,

_____

_____

_____

_____

_____

_____

_____

_____

_____

_____

_____

_____

"Most assuredly, I say to you, he who believes in Me,
the works that I do he will do also;
and greater *works* than these he will do,
because I go to My Father. And whatever you ask in My name,
that I will do, that the Father may be glorified in the Son.
If you ask anything in My name, I will do it.
Meditate on John 14:12-14

Get to know God as your Father. When you pray, call Him this—call Him Father.

Today's **WHY**

_____   _____
The Day   The Date

Dear God,

_____

_____

_____

_____

_____

_____

_____

_____

_____

_____

_____

_____

A model of how you should pray
has been left for you in the Holy Scriptures.
Jesus teaches you how to pray to Him.
He has even asked you to call him Father.
Meditate on Matthew 6:9–13

*Entrust your WHY (what hinders you) to
the Lord. He will delight you!*

Today's **WHY**

_____   _____
   The Day   The Date

Dear God,

_____
_____
_____
_____
_____
_____
_____
_____
_____
_____
_____
_____
_____

Give your life to the Lord and
He will give you the desires of your heart.
You'll be glad.
You'll be content.
You'll be delighted.
Meditate on Psalm 37:4, 5

Write down the prayers you pray to God.
The just live by faith and this too is written in the scriptures.

Today's **WHY**

_____ _____
The Day   The Date

Dear God,

_____

_____

_____

_____

_____

_____

_____

_____

_____

_____

In the Old Testament God told Moses
to write the law on two tablets of stone.
In the New Testament God declares
no prophecy of scripture is of private interpretation.
He moved holy men to write and to speak.
What these men wrote and said is still written.
Meditate on Deuteronomy 27 and 2 Peter 1

Every day take in the excellence found only in God's Word.

Today's **WHY**

_____   _____
　　　The Day　　　　　　　　　The Date

Dear God,

_____

_____

_____

_____

_____

_____

_____

_____

_____

_____

_____

_____

Are you ready to discover truth
and live an abundant life?
Meditate on Psalm 119

Trust God with your uncertainty. He is an anxiety bearer.

Today's **WHY**

_____ _____
The Day   The Date

Dear God,

_____

_____

_____

_____

_____

_____

_____

_____

_____

_____

_____

Be at ease when you're suffering.
You're in the mighty hands of God.
Meditate on 1 Peter 5:6, 7

*You've heard that His eyes rest even on
little bitty sparrows, right?*

Today's **WHY**

_____   _____
The Day   The Date

Dear God,

_____

_____

_____

_____

_____

_____

_____

_____

_____

_____

_____

_____

God knows how many hairs
you still have on your head.
Meditate on Matthew 10:27–31

The only way to find perfect peace is to pray and trust in God.

Today's **WHY**

_____	_____
The Day	The Date

Dear God,

_____

_____

_____

_____

_____

_____

_____

_____

_____

_____

_____

Are you worrying about the world or a problem?
God has already peacefully overcome
the world and your problem.
Meditate on John 16:25–33

*Invest in humble and modest behavior and
God will lift you up. He cares for you!*

Today's **WHY**

_____   _____
　　　The Day　　　　　　　　　　The Date

Dear God,

_____

_____

_____

_____

_____

_____

_____

_____

_____

_____

_____

_____

God's hand is mighty and available
to those who are humble.
Meditate on 1 Peter 5:1–7

Wait for the one who can cause you to mount up with wings as eagles.

Today's **WHY**

_____   _____
The Day   The Date

Dear God,

_____

_____

_____

_____

_____

_____

_____

_____

_____

_____

_____

_____

Wait for the one who can renew your strength,
keep you running without weariness,
keep you walking without fainting.
Meditate on Isaiah 40:31

Keep your eyes on the right man!

Today's **WHY**

_____   _____
         The Day   The Date

Dear God,

_____

_____

_____

_____

_____

_____

_____

_____

_____

_____

_____

_____

Now to Him who is able to do exceedingly
abundantly above all that we ask or think,
according to the power that works in us,
to Him be glory in the church
by Christ Jesus to all generations,
forever and ever. Amen.
Meditate on Ephesians 3:20, 21

Wisdom and understanding are profitable to you.

Today's **WHY**

_____   _____
     The Day   The Date

Dear God,

_____

_____

_____

_____

_____

_____

_____

_____

_____

_____

_____

Wisdom and understanding
are so much better than silver and gold.
Meditate on Proverbs 3:13, 14

Go ahead and seek Him. Prepare to be blessed!

Today's **WHY**

_____   _____
     The Day   The Date

Dear God,

_____

_____

_____

_____

_____

_____

_____

_____

_____

_____

_____

He's already given you the invitation to
"seek Him while He may be found."
RSVP, my dear.
Meditate on Isaiah 55:6

Keep asking. Keep seeking. Keep knocking.

Today's **WHY**

_____   _____
　　　The Day   The Date

Dear God,

_____

_____

_____

_____

_____

_____

_____

_____

_____

_____

_____

You understand you're asking,
seeking, and knocking
at the door of your Father, right?
Meditate on Matthew 7:7, 8

*Count it all joy that you cannot have the
thoughts and ways your God has!*

Today's **WHY**

_____   _____
   The Day   The Date

Dear God,

_____

_____

_____

_____

_____

_____

_____

_____

_____

_____

_____

_____

_____

"For My thoughts are not your thoughts,
nor are your ways My ways," says the Lord.
"For as the heavens are higher than the earth,
so are My ways higher than your ways,
and My thoughts than your thoughts."
Meditate on Isaiah 55:8, 9

Everything begins and ends with His unconditional love.

Today's **WHY**

_____   _____
The Day   The Date

Dear God,

_____

_____

_____

_____

_____

_____

_____

_____

_____

_____

_____

_____

Love at the beginning.
Love at the end.
Love is all you need!
Meditate on Proverbs 8:17

When the tempter comes, remember that it's not about the bread. You belong to God. Remember that it is written.

Today's **WHY**

_____   _____
　　　The Day　　　　　　　　　The Date

Dear God,

_____

_____

_____

_____

_____

_____

_____

_____	Then Jesus was led up by the Spirit into the wilderness to be tempted by the devil. And when He had fasted forty days and forty nights, afterward He was hungry. Now when the tempter came to Him, he said, "If You are the Son of God, command that these stones become bread." But He answered and said, "It is written, 'Man shall not live by bread alone, but by every word that proceeds from the mouth of God.'"

_____

_____

_____

_____

Meditate on Matthew 4:1–4

Sit still and listen. Jesus is near.

Today's **WHY**

_____   _____
         The Day   The Date

Dear God,

_____

_____

_____

_____

_____

_____

	Now it happened as they went
_____	that He entered a certain village;
	and a certain woman named Martha
	welcomed Him into her house.
_____	And she had a sister called Mary,
	who also sat at Jesus' feet and heard His word.
	But Martha was distracted with much serving,
_____	and she approached Him and said,
	"Lord, do You not care that my sister
	has left me to serve alone?
_____	Therefore tell her to help me."
	And Jesus answered and said to her,
	"Martha, Martha, you are worried
_____	and troubled about many things.
	But one thing is needed,
	and Mary has chosen that good part,
_____	which will not be taken away from her."
	Meditate on Luke 10:38–42

Are you living with the Holy Spirit?
Are you walking with the Holy Spirit?

Today's **WHY**

_____   _____
The Day   The Date

Dear God,

_____

_____

_____

_____

_____

_____

_____

_____

_____

_____

_____

_____

This is a good a day as any
to do a life-and-walk checkup.
Meditate on Galatians 5:25

No trial. No test. No gold.

Today's **WHY**

_____   _____
    The Day   The Date

Dear God,

_____

_____

_____

_____

_____

_____

_____

_____

_____

_____

_____

To have genuine faith,
you have to be tested
as if you were pure gold.
Meditate on 1 Peter 1:7, 8

Are you adding to your faith? Has it increased since the last time you checked?

Today's **WHY**

_____   _____
The Day   The Date

Dear God,

_____

_____

_____

_____

_____

_____

_____

_____

_____

_____

_____

_____

And the apostles said to the Lord,
"Increase our faith."
So the Lord said,
"If you have faith as a mustard seed,
you can say to this mulberry tree,
'Be pulled up by the roots
and be planted in the sea,'
and it would obey you."
Meditate on Luke 17:5, 6

Ask the Lord to have mercy on you.

Today's **WHY**

The Day	The Date

Dear God,

_____

_____

_____

_____

_____

_____

_____

_____

_____

_____

_____

God will pardon you too.
Meditate on Isaiah 55:7

God has smiled on you!

Today's **WHY**

_____   _____
        The Day   The Date

Dear God,

_____

_____

_____

_____

_____

_____

_____

_____

_____

_____

_____

_____

_____

> You are part of a chosen generation.
> Your priesthood is royal.
> You're from a holy nation.
> You are one of His special people.
> **Meditate on 1 Peter 2:9, 10**

God has given you a radiant, unashamed face. You are fearless.

Today's **WHY**

_____   _____
　　The Day　　　　　　　The Date

Dear God,

_____

_____

_____

_____

_____

_____

_____

_____

_____

_____

_____

Your face is radiant because you sought the Lord.
He heard you and delivered you from all your fears.
Meditate on Psalm 34:1–5

Stay alert!

Today's **WHY**

---------------   ---------------
   The Day   The Date

Dear God,

_____

_____

_____

_____

_____

_____

_____

_____

_____

_____

_____

_____

Your adversary, the devil,
is walking about like a roaring lion.
He's ready to devour you.
Meditate on 1 Peter 5:8, 9

Rejoice. Pray. Give Thanks.

Today's **WHY**

_____   _____
The Day   The Date

Dear God,

_____

_____

_____

_____

_____

_____

_____

_____

_____

_____

_____

_____

_____

_____

Do these three things.
Do them without ceasing.
Meditate on 1 Thessalonians 5:16–18

Don't stop to think about it. Come boldly to the throne of God.

Today's **WHY**

_____   _____
   The Day   The Date

Dear God,

_____

_____

_____

_____

_____

_____

_____

_____

_____

_____

_____

_____

His throne of grace holds mercy for you.
You can access that mercy anytime, anywhere.
Meditate on Hebrews 4:16

When prayers soar up, blessings rain down.

Today's **WHY**

_____   _____
        The Day   The Date

Dear God,

_____

_____

_____

_____

_____

_____

_____

_____

_____

_____

_____

Prayer is a conversation with an able God. He can make grace and mercy surround you and do so much more. Write this blessing down.
Meditate on 2 Corinthians 9:8

You were born for life's battles. This is not the best news.
You are equipped to win these battles. This is the blessed news.
Listen up! God and Satan are simply not equal.

Today's **WHY**

_____   _____
      The Day   The Date

Dear God,

_____

_____

_____

_____

_____

_____

_____

_____

_____

_____

_____

_____

_____

God versus Satan.
No problem.
Meditate on 1 John 4:4

Stay in His healing presence.

Today's **WHY**

_____   _____
   The Day   The Date

Dear God,

_____

_____

_____

_____

_____

_____

_____

_____

_____

_____

_____

Trust me. There is balm in Gilead
and there's a physician there.
Meditate on Jeremiah 8:21, 22

All day long let your life reflect the transforming God you serve.

Today's **WHY**

The Day	The Date

Dear God,

_____

_____

_____

_____

_____

_____

_____

_____

_____

_____

_____

_____

You can be a new person
because of your renewed mind.
God is able to transform your thinking.
Meditate on Romans 12:2

You cannot beat God at anything. Especially giving.

Today's **WHY**

_____   _____
     The Day   The Date

Dear God,

_____

_____

_____

_____

_____

_____

_____

_____

_____

_____

_____

God gave you His very best—
His only begotten Son.
You had access to this giving God
even before you believed He was God.
Meditate on John 3:15

The more you know and experience God, the more you'll trust that He'll hide you in the time of trouble and set you high on a rock.

Today's **WHY**

_____   _____
The Day   The Date

Dear God,

_____

_____

_____

_____

_____

_____

_____

_____

_____

_____

_____

_____

_____

_____

HE IS there for you in times of trouble.
Meditate on Psalm 27:5

God stays the same while everything else changes.

Today's **WHY**

_____   _____
The Day   The Date

Dear God,

_____

_____

_____

_____

_____

_____

_____

_____

_____

_____

_____

Yesterday, today, tomorrow—
same God.
Meditate on James 1:17

Faith makes hindrances flee—Satan included.

Today's **WHY**

_____   _____
The Day   The Date

Dear God,

_____

_____

_____

_____

_____

_____

_____

_____

_____

_____

_____

_____

Submit to God.
Resist the devil.
He will flee.
Meditate on James 4:7, 8

Tribulation produces perseverance, and perseverance, character…

Today's **WHY**

_____   _____
The Day   The Date

Dear God,

_____

_____

_____

_____

_____

_____

_____

_____

_____

_____

_____

… and character, hope.
Meditate on Romans 5:1–5

You do not have enough power to defeat the multitude.

Today's **WHY**

_____   _____
   The Day   The Date

Dear God,

_____
_____
_____
_____
_____
_____
_____
_____
_____
_____
_____
_____
_____
_____

God does!
Meditate on 2 Chronicles 20:12

God goes to the fight ahead of you.

Today's **WHY**

_____   _____
          The Day   The Date

Dear God,

_____

_____

_____

_____

_____

_____

_____

_____

_____

_____

_____

_____

Any questions?
Meditate on Deuteronomy 20:4

Stay strong!

Today's **WHY**

---------------   ---------------
The Day   The Date

Dear God,

_____

_____

_____

_____

_____

_____

_____

_____

_____

_____

_____

_____

_____

"I've got this."
—God
Meditate on Isaiah 40:29

Did you realize that leaning on Jesus gives you access to His understanding rather than yours?

Today's **WHY**

_____   _____
The Day   The Date

Dear God,

_____

_____

_____

_____

_____

_____

_____

_____

_____

_____

Trust in the Lord with all your heart,
and lean not on your own understanding.
Meditate on Proverbs 3:5

Have you acknowledged Jesus in every way?

Today's **WHY**

_____   _____
   The Day   The Date

Dear God,

_____

_____

_____

_____

_____

_____

_____

_____

_____

_____

_____

He'll direct your path.
Meditate on Proverbs 3:6

God is greater than anything in this old world.

Today's **WHY**

_____   _____
       The Day   The Date

Dear God,

_____

_____

_____

_____

_____

_____

_____

_____

_____

_____

Enough said!
Meditate on 1 John 4:4

WRITE IT TO **GOD**.

Today's **WHY**

_____ _____
    The Day   The Date

Dear God,

_____

_____

_____

_____

_____

_____

_____

_____

_____

_____

_____

_____

He's ready to respond.
He already heard your WHY.
Meditate on Jeremiah 29:11–12

Seek Him and you will find Him.

Today's **WHY**

_____   _____
The Day   The Date

Dear God,

_____

_____

_____

_____

_____

_____

_____

_____

_____

_____

_____

_____

_____

You will find Him when you
search with all your heart.
Meditate on Jeremiah 29:13

You are next, right after His angels.

Today's **WHY**

_____ _____
The Day The Date

Dear God,

_____

_____

_____

_____

_____

_____

_____

_____

_____

_____

_____

He's forever mindful of you.
Meditate on Psalm 8:4, 5

Be a blessing.

Today's **WHY**

_____   _____
The Day   The Date

Dear God,

_____

_____

_____

_____

_____

_____

_____

_____

_____

_____

_____

Trust in the Lord.
Hope in the Lord.
Meditate on Jeremiah 17:7, 8

Doubt and unbelief are a normal part of the trust process.
We go through doubt on the way to being
able to truly trust in the Lord.

Today's **WHY**

_____   _____
   The Day   The Date

Dear God,

_____
_____
_____
_____
_____
_____
_____
_____
_____
_____
_____
_____
_____
_____

God never fails us.
His timing may be different than we expect.
He simply has not and cannot fail to be on time.
Meditate on John 20:26, 27

Are you fully dressed?

Today's **WHY**

_____   _____
　　The Day　　　　　　　　　　The Date

Dear God,

_____

_____

_____

_____

_____

_____

_____

_____

_____

_____

_____

_____

Are you wearing the whole armor of God yet?
Meditate on Ephesians 6:10–13

Is your heart and your thinking protected?

Today's **WHY**

_____ _____
The Day   The Date

Dear God,

_____

_____

_____

_____

_____

_____

_____

_____

_____

_____

_____

Get your breastplate.
Gird it around your waist.
Meditate on Ephesians 6:14

Is your faith with you? Are your shoes on?

Today's **WHY**

_____   _____
The Day   The Date

Dear God,

_____

_____

_____

_____

_____

_____

_____

_____

_____

_____

_____

Show me your shield, please.
Meditate on Ephesians 6:15, 16

Protect your mind and your thoughts with the helmet of salvation.

Today's **WHY**

The Day   The Date

Dear God,

_____

_____

_____

_____

_____

_____

_____

_____

_____

_____

_____

_____

Play defense.
Do you have the Word of God
which is your spiritual sword?
Meditate on Ephesians 6:17

*God's peace and the witnesses compassed about
you will beat down your WHY every time.*

Today's **WHY**

    _____   _____
         The Day   The Date

Dear God,

_____

_____

_____

_____

_____

_____

_____

_____

_____

_____

_____

Go on! Give "what hinders you" to God.
Meditate on Hebrews 12:1

You are all the endorsement that's needed.
Your very life is a letter that anyone can read when
they look at you. Christ himself wrote about this.

Today's **WHY**

_____   _____
    The Day   The Date

Dear God,

_____

_____

_____

_____

_____

_____

_____

_____

_____

_____

_____ Are we beginning to commend ourselves again?
                   Or do we need, as some do,
                   letters of recommendation to you or from you?
                   You yourselves are our letter of recommendation,
_____ written on our hearts, to be known and read by all.
                   And you show that you are a letter from Christ
                   delivered by us, written not with ink
                   but with the Spirit of the living God,
                   not on tablets of stone but on tablets of human hearts.
                   Meditate on 2 Corinthians 3:1–3

Dear Heart, God is speaking to you right now.

Today's **WHY**

_____   _____
The Day   The Date

Dear God,

_____

_____

_____

_____

_____

_____

_____

_____

_____

_____

_____

_____

With your whole heart opened,
read the words in the fortieth chapter of Isaiah.
Study Isaiah 40

There is so much to say amen to right now.

Today's **WHY**

_____   _____
         The Day   The Date

Dear God,

_____

_____

_____

_____

_____

_____

_____

_____

_____

_____

_____

_____

_____

But may the God of all grace,
who called us to His eternal glory by Christ Jesus,
after you have suffered awhile, perfect,
establish, strengthen, and settle you.
To Him be the glory and the dominion
forever and ever. Amen.
Meditate on 1 Peter 5:10, 11

The Lord IS your shepherd. While you were about nothing,
He was about the business of caring for you.

Today's **WHY**

_____   _____
        The Day   The Date

Dear God,

_____

_____

_____

_____

_____

_____

_____

_____

_____

_____

_____

_____

The Lord is my shepherd; I shall not want.
Meditate on Psalm 23:1

He lies you down in safe, still places.

Today's **WHY**

_____   _____
     The Day   The Date

Dear God,

_____

_____

_____

_____

_____

_____

_____

_____

_____

_____

_____

He makes me to lie down in green pastures;
He leads me beside the still waters.
Meditate on Psalm 23:2

*Spending time with God restores you soul
and makes your path right.*

Today's **WHY**

_____   _____
　　The Day　　　　　　　　The Date

Dear God,

_____

_____

_____

_____

_____

_____

_____

_____

_____

_____

_____

He restores my soul;
He leads me in the paths of righteousness
For His name's sake.
Meditate on Psalm 23:3

God helps you overcome your fears and comforts you.

Today's **WHY**

_____   _____
          The Day   The Date

Dear God,

_____

_____

_____

_____

_____

_____

_____

_____

_____

_____

_____

_____

> Yea, though I walk through the valley of the shadow of death,
> I will fear no evil; For You *are* with me;
> Your rod and Your staff, they comfort me
> ***Meditate on Psalm 23:4***

*God provides for you in front of your enemies' faces.
Tell somebody!*

Today's **WHY**

_____   _____
　　The Day　　　　　　　　The Date

Dear God,

_____

_____

_____

_____

_____

_____

_____

_____

_____

_____

You prepare a table before me in the presence of my enemies;
You anoint my head with oil; My cup runs over.
Meditate on Psalm 23:5

God, who brings goodness and mercy, will give you a dwelling place forevermore.

Today's **WHY**

_____   _____
       The Day   The Date

Dear God,

_____

_____

_____

_____

_____

_____

_____

_____

_____

_____

_____

_____

_____

_____

Surely goodness and mercy shall follow me
All the days of my life;
And I will dwell
in the house of the Lord Forever.
Meditate on Psalm 23:6

You are a living stone. He is the cornerstone that's chief.

Today's **WHY**

_____   _____
　　The Day   The Date

Dear God,

_____

_____

_____

_____

_____

_____

_____

_____

_____   Coming to Him *as* to a living stone,
                              rejected indeed by men,
                          but chosen by God *and* precious,
                              you also, as living stones,
_____   are being built up a spiritual house,
                                 a holy priesthood,
                            to offer up spiritual sacrifices
                        acceptable to God through Jesus Christ.
_____ Therefore it is also contained in the Scripture,
                       "Behold, I lay in Zion A chief cornerstone,
                         elect, precious, and he who believes on Him
                             will by no means be put to shame.
_____   ***Meditate on 1 Peter 2:4-6***

You now have a power source. Your power source is the Holy Spirit. Claim it!

Today's **WHY**

_____   _____
            The Day   The Date

Dear God,

_____

_____

_____

_____

_____

_____

_____

_____

_____

_____

_____

_____

Now may the God of hope fill you with all joy
and peace in believing,
that you may abound in hope
by the power of the Holy Spirit.
Meditate on Romans 15:13

The Lord's eyes and ears are open to you who are righteous. He pays attention.

Today's **WHY**

_____   _____
　　　The Day　　　　　　　　　The Date

Dear God,

_____

_____

_____

_____

_____

_____

_____

_____

_____

_____

The eyes of the Lord are on the righteous
and His ears are open to their cry.
Meditate on Psalm 34:15

*All those hindrances surrounding you right
now are working for your good.*

Today's **WHY**

_____   _____
The Day   The Date

Dear God,

_____

_____

_____

_____

_____

_____

_____

_____

_____

_____

_____

_____

God will give your troubles purpose.
Meditate on Romans 8:28

Able? Actually, He's more than able.

Today's **WHY**

_____   _____
The Day   The Date

Dear God,

_____

_____

_____

_____

_____

_____

_____

_____

_____

_____

_____

Pray to this more-than-able one.
Meditate on Jude 1:24, 25

God says you are salt and light.

Today's **WHY**

_____   _____
          The Day   The Date

Dear God,

_____

_____

_____

_____

_____

_____

_____

_____

_____

_____

_____

God says salt and light cannot be hidden.
Meditate on Matthew 5:13–15

*You can live a life that is not "puffed up"
since shortly, God is coming to you.*

Today's **WHY**

_____   _____
         The Day   The Date

Dear God,

_____

_____

_____

_____

_____

_____

_____

_____

_____   Now some are puffed up, as though
                            I were not coming to you.
                            But I will come to you shortly,
_____   if the Lord wills, and I will know,
                           not the word of those who are puffed up,
                            but the power. For the kingdom of God
_____   is not in word but in power.
                                      What do you want?
                                Shall I come to you with a rod,
_____   or in love and a spirit of gentleness?
                           Meditate on 1 Corinthians 4:18–21

The Lord has His eye on those who are righteous.

Today's **WHY**

_____   _____
The Day   The Date

Dear God,

_____

_____

_____

_____

_____

_____

_____

_____

_____

_____

_____

His ears will hear your cry.
Meditate on Psalm 34:15

*Continuing His good work in you is just another
one of the plans God has for you.*

Today's **WHY**

_____   _____
   The Day   The Date

Dear God,

_____

_____

_____

_____

_____

_____

_____

_____

_____

_____

_____

You are a work in progress.
God will complete you.
Meditate on Philippians 1:3–6

Make your singing joyful and filled with praise.

Today's **WHY**

_____   _____
　　The Day　　　　　　　　　　　The Date

Dear God,

_____

_____

_____

_____

_____

_____

_____

_____

_____

_____

_____

Sing and be happy today.
Meditate on Psalm 100:1–3

Relax when you are experiencing fear.

Today's **WHY**

_____   _____
     The Day   The Date

Dear God,

_____

_____

_____

_____

_____

_____

_____

_____

_____

_____

God holds you in His safe right hand.
Meditate on Isaiah 41:10

Have you begun your healing?

Today's **WHY**

_____   _____
The Day   The Date

Dear God,

_____

_____

_____

_____

_____

_____

_____

_____

_____

_____

_____

_____

Be anxious for nothing,
but in everything
by prayer and supplication,
with thanksgiving,
let your requests be made
known to God; and the peace of God,
which surpasses all understanding,
will guard your hearts
and minds through Christ Jesus.
Meditate on Philippians 4:6–7

Do not let anything stop you now!

Today's **WHY**

_____   _____
The Day   The Date

Dear God,

_____

_____

_____

_____

_____

_____

_____

_____

_____

_____

_____

_____

Rejoice!
God's got your WHY in the palm of His hand.
Meditate on Philippians 4:4–7

Beloved, did you know keeping God's commandments is a commandment from God Himself?
You do now.

Today's **WHY**

_____   _____
The Day   The Date

Dear God,

_____

_____

_____

_____

_____

_____

_____

_____

_____

_____

                    "Beware that you do not forget the Lord your God
                    by not keeping His commandments, His judgments,
_____   and His statutes which I command you today....
                    Meditate on Deuteronomy 8:11

                    Circumcision is nothing and uncircumcision is nothing,
_____   but keeping the commandments of God is what matters.
                    Meditate on 1 Corinthians 7:19

Allow God's love to go deep inside you.
He knows every small and large hindered part of you.
Let the light of His love shine on your hurts and you will heal.

Today's **WHY**

_____   _____
The Day   The Date

Dear God,

_____

_____

_____

_____

_____

_____

_____

_____

_____

_____

_____

Let the power of His love surround your sadness.
Sadness will flee.
God's answers for you are deep and wide.
Meditate on Psalm 139:1–5

Just like Jeremiah, search for Him with all of your heart.

Today's **WHY**

_____   _____
     The Day   The Date

Dear God,

_____

_____

_____

_____

_____

_____

_____

_____

_____

_____

_____

_____

It's you responsibility to seek Him.
Meditate on Jeremiah 29:13

*Expect blessings when you put your hope
and confidence in the Lord.*

Today's **WHY**

_____   _____
   The Day   The Date

Dear God,

_____

_____

_____

_____

_____

_____

_____

_____

_____

_____

_____

_____

Are you expecting your blessings yet?
Meditate on Jeremiah 17:7

It's time for your transformation to begin.

Today's **WHY**

_____   _____
      The Day   The Date

Dear God,

_____

_____

_____

_____

_____

_____

_____

_____

_____

_____

And do not be conformed to this world,
but be transformed by the renewing of your mind,
that you may prove what *is* that good
and acceptable and perfect will of God.
Meditate on Romans 12:2

*Read God's Word and discover your unique
and perfect spiritual gifts,*

Today's **WHY**

_____   _____
         The Day   The Date

Dear God,

_____

_____

_____

_____

_____

_____

_____

_____

…God has dealt to each one a measure of faith.
For as we have many members in one body,
but all the members do not have the same function,
so we, *being* many, are one body in Christ,
and individually members of one another.
Having then gifts differing
according to the grace that is given to us…
Meditate on Romans 12:3a-6a

*The Lord has beautiful, timely gifts to give to you.
Are you ready to receive them?*

Today's **WHY**

_____   _____
   The Day   The Date

Dear God,

_____

_____

_____

_____

_____

_____

_____

_____

_____

_____

_____

_____

He has made everything beautiful in its time.
Also He has put eternity in their hearts,
except that no one can find out the work
that God does from beginning to end.
I know that nothing is better for them than to rejoice,
and to do good in their lives,
and also that every man should eat
and drink and enjoy the good of all his labor—
it is the gift of God.
Meditate on Ecclesiastes 3:11–13

Pray with me, please.

Today's **WHY**

_____   _____
         The Day   The Date

Dear God,

_____

_____

_____

_____

_____

_____

_____

_____

_____

_____

Father God,
please let all my prayers be humble
and acceptable to you.
Meditate on 1 Peter 2:5

Expect the miracle of a long life.

Today's **WHY**

_____   _____
The Day   The Date

Dear God,

_____

_____

_____

_____

_____

_____

_____

_____

_____

_____

Read what God has written in
Proverbs 3:1–2

You'll experience plenty when you give your first fruits to God.

Today's **WHY**

_____   _____
The Day   The Date

Dear God,

_____

_____

_____

_____

_____

_____

_____

_____

_____

_____

_____

The Lord will make your barns overflow.
Meditate on Proverbs 3:9, 10

Stay extraordinary.

Today's **WHY**

_____   _____
   The Day   The Date

Dear God,

_____

_____

_____

_____

_____

_____

_____

_____

_____

_____

_____

_____

You can stay extraordinary if you stay with the Lord.
Meditate on Ephesians 2:10

The Holy Spirit "goggles" on your behalf.

Today's **WHY**

_____   _____
   The Day   The Date

Dear God,

_____

_____

_____

_____

_____

_____

_____

_____

_____

_____

_____

_____

He's the best search engine intercessor you will ever find.
Meditate on Jeremiah 17:10

*Are you weak? He'll give you power and
then renew your strength.*

Today's **WHY**

_____   _____
   The Day   The Date

Dear God,

_____

_____

_____

_____

_____

_____

_____

_____

_____   He gives power to the weak,
                             and to those who have no might
                                  He increases strength.
_____   Even the youths shall faint and be weary,
                             and the young men shall utterly fall,
                              but those who wait on the Lord
_____   shall renew their strength;
                         they shall mount up with wings like eagles,
                               they shall run and not be weary,
_____   they shall walk and not faint.
                                  Meditate on Isaiah 40:29–31

Who and what gets your time?

Today's **WHY**

_____ _____
The Day   The Date

Dear God,

_____

_____

_____

_____

_____

_____

_____

_____

_____

_____

Pay close spiritual attention
as you write down
today's WHY.
Hindrances should be clearer now.
Meditate on 2 Corinthians 6:14–15

Get your house in order.
This is a spiritual not a physical command.

Today's **WHY**

_____   _____
    The Day   The Date

Dear God,

_____

_____

_____

_____

_____

_____

_____

_____

_____

_____

_____

_____

And again I say, get your house in order.
Do it this day!
Meditate on Joshua 24:15

Do you believe what you read in the Holy Scriptures?
Do you?

Today's **WHY**

———————   ———————
The Day   The Date

Dear God,

_____

_____

_____

_____

_____

_____

_____

_____

_____

_____

_____

_____

Do you understand what you read?
Meditate on 2 Chronicles 20:20

No soaring pain. No spiritual gain.

Today's **WHY**

——————————— ———————————
The Day   The Date

Dear God,

_____

_____

_____

_____

_____

_____

_____

_____

———————————————

———————————————

———————————————

———————————————

Consider it pure joy,
my brothers and sisters, whenever
you face trials of many kinds,
because you know that
the testing of your faith produces
perseverance. Let perseverance
finish its work so that you may
be mature and complete,
not lacking anything.
Meditate on James 1:2–4

Rock steady!

Today's **WHY**

_____   _____
          The Day   The Date

Dear God,

_____

_____

_____

_____

_____

_____

_____

_____

_____

_____

_____

Dear Heart,
you have what you need to make your rock steady.
Meditate on Philippians 4:11–13

You must run and tell others about Christ's answers to your WHY.

Today's **WHY**

The Day	The Date

Dear God,

_____

_____

_____

_____

_____

_____

_____

_____

_____

_____

_____

_____

Don't leave anyone out.
Tell everybody.
Study Colossians 3

*I'm sure I mentioned earlier that God has
you in the palm of His hand.*

Today's **WHY**

_____   _____
   The Day   The Date

Dear God,

_____

_____

_____

_____

_____

_____

_____

_____

_____

_____

_____

He has your WHY there too.
Meditate on Psalm 139:5

Bless the Lord at all times.

Today's **WHY**

_____   _____
The Day   The Date

Dear God,

_____

_____

_____

_____

_____

_____

_____

_____

_____

_____

_____

_____

Keep His praise continually in your mouth.
Meditate on Psalm 34:1

Let your soul make its boast in the Lord.
When you're humble you'll clearly hear His answers.

Today's **WHY**

_____   _____
         The Day   The Date

Dear God,

_____

_____

_____

_____

_____

_____

_____

_____

_____

_____

_____

_____

Only the Lord can free you from fear, deliver you from trouble, supply all your needs, listen to you at all times, and show you great kindness. You can boast here and the humble shall hear of you.
Meditate on Psalm 34:2

Have you really sought the Lord?
Have you?

Today's **WHY**

_____   _____
The Day   The Date

Dear God,

_____

_____

_____

_____

_____

_____

_____

_____

_____

_____

_____

He will deliver you from all your fears.
Meditate on Psalm 34:4

Do you know what Job knows?

Today's **WHY**

_____   _____
   The Day   The Date

Dear God,

_____
_____
_____
_____
_____
_____
_____
_____
_____
_____
_____
_____

Do you know that the Lord can do anything?
Did you know that what He has purposed for you
cannot be withheld from you?
Job knows.
Meditate on Job 42:1–2

*Stay in constant contact with the Lord.
Call Him by name when your mind drifts
toward what hinders you.*

Today's **WHY**

_____ _____
The Day   The Date

Dear God,

_____

_____

_____

_____

_____

_____

_____

_____

_____

_____

The Lord will capture your thoughts.
The Lord will equip you for the rest of your journey.
Meditate on Exodus 33:12–14

Are you in a storm or just out of one?
Are you heading into a storm?
God's guidance is what you need.

Today's **WHY**

_____   _____
       The Day   The Date

Dear God,

_____

_____

_____

_____

_____

_____

_____

_____

_____

_____

_____

Storms will come.
Study Psalm 5

*Do you need God to read what you've written
early in the morning?
No problem.*

Today's **WHY**

_____   _____
The Day   The Date

Dear God,

_____

_____

_____

_____

_____

_____

_____

_____

_____

_____

_____

_____

God is up before you get up every morning.
Meditate on Psalm 5:3

*You are not surrounded just by your WHY.
A great cloud of witnesses also surrounds you.*

Today's **WHY**

_____   _____
           The Day   The Date

Dear God,

_____

_____

_____

_____

_____

_____

_____

_____

_____

_____

_____

_____

Lift up your head.
You'll come face to face with God,
the perfector of your faith.
Meditate on Hebrews 12:1–2

Are you saved?
Do not be boastful about your salvation.

Today's **WHY**

_____   _____
   The Day   The Date

Dear God,

_____

_____

_____

_____

_____

_____

_____

_____

_____

_____

_____

_____

_____

Your salvation is a gift from God.
Meditate on Ephesians 2:8–10

What you get depends on what you're doing.

Today's **WHY**

_____   _____
The Day   The Date

Dear God,

_____

_____

_____

_____

_____

_____

_____

_____

_____

_____

_____

> I, the Lord, search the heart,
> I try the reins, even to give
> every man according to his ways,
> and according to the fruit
> of his doings.
> ***Meditate on Jeremiah 17:10***

I say it again, don't stop to think about it.
Come boldly to the throne of God.

Today's **WHY**

_____ _____
The Day   The Date

Dear God,

_____
_____
_____
_____
_____
_____
_____
_____
_____
_____
_____
_____

For we have not an high priest which cannot
be touched with the feeling of our infirmities;
but was in all points tempted like as we are, yet without sin.
Let us therefore come boldly unto the throne of grace,
that we may obtain mercy,
and find grace to help in time of need.
Meditate on Hebrews 4:15, 16

You know there is a great gap between your thoughts and the Lord's thoughts, right?

Today's **WHY**

_____   _____
          The Day   The Date

Dear God,

_____

_____

_____

_____

_____

_____

_____

_____

	Let the wicked forsake his way,
_____	and the unrighteous man his thoughts:
_____	and let him return unto the Lord, and he will have mercy upon him; and to our God,
_____	for he will abundantly pardon. For my thoughts are not your thoughts,
_____	neither are your ways my ways, saith the Lord.

Meditate on Isaiah 55:7–8

Don't worry about anything; pray about everything;
be thankful; make your requests known to God.

Today's **WHY**

_____   _____
The Day   The Date

Dear God,

_____

_____

_____

_____

_____

_____

_____

_____

_____

_____

_____

_____

Be anxious for nothing,
but in everything by prayer and supplication,
with thanksgiving, let your requests be made known to God;
and the peace of God, which surpasses all understanding,
will guard your hearts and minds through Christ Jesus.
Meditate on Philippians 4:6, 7

After learning what's true, noble, just, pure, lovely, and of good report — meditate — then do!

Today's **WHY**

_____ _____
        The Day   The Date

Dear God,

_____

_____

_____

_____

_____

_____

_____

_____

_____

_____   Finally, brethren,
                           whatever things are true,
                           whatever things are noble,
_____   whatever things are just,
                           whatever things are pure,
                           whatever things are lovely,
                           whatever things are of good report,
                           if there is any virtue
_____   and if there is anything praiseworthy—
                           meditate on these things.
                           Apply Philippians 4:8

After you learn, receive, hear, and see,
— meditate — then do!

Today's **WHY**

_____   _____
   The Day   The Date

Dear God,

_____

_____

_____

_____

_____

_____

_____

_____

_____

_____

_____

_____

The God of peace will be with you.
Meditate on Philippians 4: 9

Look to Jesus. He gives you your faith. He makes it perfect. He did not give up on you. Don't you give up on you either.

Today's **WHY**

_____ _____
    The Day   The Date

Dear God,

_____

_____

_____

_____

_____

_____

_____

_____

_____

_____

_____

_____

God is preparing a place for those who remain obedient to His Word.
Meditate on Hebrews 1:2

Obedience to God's Word brings peace.

Today's **WHY**

_____   _____
The Day   The Date

Dear God,

_____

_____

_____

_____

_____

_____

_____

_____

_____

_____

_____

_____

Don't you dare worry about a thing!
Meditate on Philippians 4:6–7

*Who is in control of your WHY—
you or the great I AM?*

Today's **WHY**

_____   _____
    The Day   The Date

Dear God,

_____

_____

_____

_____

_____

_____

_____	Then Moses said to God,
	"Indeed, when I come
	to the children of Israel
_____	and say to them,
	'The God of your fathers
	has sent me to you,'
_____	and they say to me,
	'What is His name?'
	what shall I say to them?"
_____	And God said to Moses,
	"I AM WHO I AM."
	And He said,
_____	"Thus you shall say
	to the children of Israel,
	'I AM has sent me to you.'"
_____	**Study Exodus 3**

God has made plans for you for such a time as this.

Today's **WHY**

_____   _____
       The Day   The Date

Dear God,

_____

_____

_____

_____

_____

_____

_____

_____

_____

_____

_____

The plans God has made for you
are more than you would ever
consider asking Him for.
Meditate on Jeremiah 29:11

*Meditate on God's Word.
It's filled with good and perfect gifts from above.*

Today's **WHY**

_____   _____
   The Day   The Date

Dear God,

_____

_____

_____

_____

_____

_____

_____

_____

_____

_____

_____

_____

Every good gift and every perfect gift is from above,
and comes down from the Father of lights,
with whom there is no variation or shadow of turning.
Of His own will He brought us forth by the word of truth,
that we might be a kind of first fruits of His creatures
Meditate on James 1:17, 18

Do you know what to do first to begin your healing?

Today's **WHY**

_____   _____
The Day   The Date

Dear God,

_____

_____

_____

_____

_____

_____

_____

_____

_____

_____

_____

_____

> But seek first the kingdom of God and His righteousness,
> and all these things shall be added to you.
> ***Apply Matthew 6:33***

First,
don't worry about a thing.

Today's **WHY**

_____ _____
　　The Day　　　　　　　　The Date

Dear God,

_____

_____

_____

_____

_____

_____

_____

_____

_____

_____

_____

_____

…do not worry about tomorrow,
for tomorrow will worry about its own things.
Sufficient for the day *is* its own trouble.
Apply Matthew 6:34

I'm in prayer, asking God to begin your healing today.
This hopeful prayer of mine is continuous.
God has perfect knowledge of you.

Today's **WHY**

_____   _____
The Day   The Date

Dear God,

_____

_____

_____

_____

_____

_____

_____

_____   Pray with me, please …
Heavenly Father, thank You
for Your unconditional love,
for loving me while I was yet
a sinner, and for holding me
_____   in the palms of Your hands.
Please help me know You
more intimately. Help me
_____   turn to You more often.
Help me to take every failure,
every disappointment, and
every struggle to You
_____   more immediately! Help me to
always talk to You through
my prayers, my praise, and
_____   my writings.
Study Psalm 139

O Lord, You have searched me and known me.
You know my sitting down and my rising up;
    You understand my thought afar off.
You comprehend my path and my lying down,
    And are acquainted with all my ways.
    For there is not a word on my tongue,
But behold, O Lord, You know it altogether.
Meditate on Psalm 139:1–4

Have you ever thought about writing down your blessings rather than your sorrows?

Now that you've completed this round of writings to God. Now that your healing has begun,

Write down your blessings—
Write down each and every one.
Write down every blessing, then
Share what God has done!

Order your first DELIVERANCE *Diary* at www.thenewleafmedia.com and major booksellers such as: Barnes & Nobles, Amazon, eBay, etc.

DELIVERANCE *Diary*
Write down every blessing.
Date Begun _____
Day Begun _____

About the Author

It's about giving flowers ...

Since forever, we've heard our families and friends say, "Give me my flowers while I'm living." It is these words that inspired the creation of a line of greeting cards, books, and Christian products we call *a few flowers*™.

We offer elegant, limited edition, handmade cards written to encourage, inspire, strengthen, and assure.

There are Christian books that will help you heal and products that will delight you in a mighty way.
Look us over at afewlowers.com.

Dearly Beloved,
The flowers are in the words.
The words are the flowers
that are being given to you.
My goal is to give you
your flowers while you're living.
Therefore, here are
a few flowers™
from me to you.

©2005 *a few flowers*™. This business concept and all products are registered trademarks. All right reserved.

Write Your Letters to God.

E. J. H. MOFFETT EVANS is a member of the Church of Christ at East Side in Austin, Texas.

She has an associate's degree in arts from Austin Community College, a bachelor's degree in journalism from the University of Texas at Austin, and a master of liberal arts degree from St. Edwards University, all located in Austin, Texas. She has owned her Christian greeting card company, *a few flowers*™, since 2005. She also creates documents and handles communications for her church.

Erma has been prayerfully and compassionately studying the Word of God for more than thirty-five years. Grounded in her study and understanding of the scriptures, her elegant, limited-edition Christian greeting cards continue to encourage, inspire, strengthen, and assure her customers. In addition, she has always written down her prayers to God.

This book gives you space to capture your daily thoughts in letters to God. Erma's goal has been to offer flowers to those she meets on her journey, and you will find flowers every time you write in this spiritual healing journal.

This is no little bitty God you're writing to. He sits on high yet He is always at your side. All of your problems can be contained and dealt within the palm of His hand.

Do not worry about your tomorrow. Throw off this unfair burden once and for all. Seek God's above all else. This will bring you directly into His presence. Hindrances will flee. Healing will begin.

Everything you need is in His church.

The Scripture Passage That Began My Journey But seek first the kingdom of God and his righteousness, and all these things will be added to you. "Therefore do not be anxious about tomorrow, for tomorrow will be anxious for itself. Sufficient for the day is its own trouble.
Meditate on Matthew 6:33, 34 ESV

But seek first his kingdom and his righteousness, and all these things will be given to you as well. Therefore do not worry about tomorrow, for tomorrow will worry about itself. Each day has enough trouble of its own.
Meditate on Matthew 6:33, 34 NIV

But seek ye first the kingdom of God, and his righteousness; and all these things shall be added unto you. Take therefore no thought for the morrow: or the morrow shall take thought for the things of itself. Sufficient unto the day is the evil thereof.
Meditate on Matthew 6:33, 34 KJV

www.ingramcontent.com/pod-product-compliance
Lightning Source LLC
Chambersburg PA
CBHW071855070526
44583CB00016B/1696